Living In Faith

A 90-Day Devotional
By Marshall Armstrong

Acknowledgments

I am so excited to share another part of my life with you. This is a devotional journal through rhyming poems. My ultimate prayer is that God would speak to you through these simple words.

I would like to thank my reviewers, editors, and all the other people in my life that provided encouragement and inspiration. There are many friends and family that made this possible by providing their unwavering support, inspiration, wisdom, and advice.

Other titles by Marshall Armstrong

Timeless Poetry

Follow Marshall Armstrong

Facebook

Instagram

Special Thanks

Thank you so much for joining in on this 90-day journey. If you are looking for a quick 5-8 minute devotion to start the day, or plan to spend 15-20 minutes interacting with the poems and verses, this is the place for you. Before we jump right into day one, take a few minutes and make the following commitments. Afterall, if we make a commitment, we are more likely to complete the journey.

I commit to spending the following time every day in this devotional: (i.e. 6:00am, 5:00pm, 8:30pm)

_____

I commit to doing this devotional with: (i.e. self, family, small group)

_____

I commit to praying that God will open my heart to what He would have me learn: (write out a short prayer of openness and commitment here)

_____

_____

_____

_____

_____

Start each day with a short prayer asking God to reveal Himself to you. Ask Him to show you what He wants you to know and how you can apply what you have learned. Sometimes you already have the experience or knowledge of the concept presented, so some days may just be a reinforcement of what you know. Use those days as a time to recommit to the application presented.

Throughout the 90-days, each devotion begins with a poem. After you have read the poem, there are Bible verses for you to look up and read. Please take the time to read the short passages or verses. After all, the Word of God is better than any words of a human.

After the verses, there are some thought provoking questions for you to consider and answer. There is some space provided to write in the book. Use the margins and blank spaces to complete your thoughts, ideas, and lessons learned.

Thanks again for joining me on this 90-day journey!

Poems

8

Intimacy With God

There is a place we desire to be-
where all is known, complete intimacy.

God knows every going and coming-
where all is laid bare and there is no judging.

He knows the sin and shame-
and still calls us by name.

Where we are recognized individually-
here is this perfect intimacy.

A love that is never-ending-
this invitation He is always sending.

Even with all our wrongs and flaws-
we get to experience intimacy with God.

Read:

- James 4:8
- Psalm 73:28

What does intimacy with God look like for you?

_____

_____

_____

_____

_____

What barriers or distractions may be preventing you from intimacy with God?

_____

_____

_____

_____

_____

_____

_____

Pray that God would draw near to you over these next 90 days. Write a little about what you might want to experience during this time.

_____

_____

_____

_____

_____

_____

_____

_____

These Simple Words

Sometimes I can't find the right words to say.
I try to speak Your love, but it comes out the wrong way.

I try to find the right voice to communicate-
to the world in a way that shows Your love and grace.

These words are small and insufficient.
Lacking in every way, knowing they are not enough.

Reaching back to any simple word I could find-
attempting to describe Your perfect life.

So make these simple words express-
all Your wonderful Holiness.

Allow my words to touch Your people.
Even though these words are inadequate and simple.

Read:

- Matthew 10:20
- John 14:26

Is it comforting to know that God gives us the Holy Spirit who will speak through us? How so?

_____

_____

_____

_____

How does that realization help you tell others about God's love in your life?

_____

_____

_____

_____

_____

_____

_____

_____

_____

Pray God will give you the opportunity to share His lovewith someone in the next 90 days. Write out that prayer.

_____

_____

_____

_____

_____

_____

_____

_____

Let's Talk

Why is it?
I talk.
You listen.
I don't stop.

"Dear Jesus, I need this, and I want that.
And I want healing for the folks in my family.
Thanks for listening to all I ask.
I think that's it for now, thanks for listening to me."

No interruption.
You wait.
This conversation.
Is all one way.

It's then that I realize I did all the talking.
I did not stop to hear what You would say.
Not once was I still to do any listening.
I did all the talking every time I prayed.

Yet still, You waited patiently-
staying with me all the while-
smiling down as I babble on endlessly-

My focus shifts, be still and know,
You are God and I am not.
I sit at Your feet; quiet, humble.

I apologize.
Own my mistake.
I realize.
You already forgave.

I sit and wait for You to speak.
Intently listening. Silently.
I see You look down my way-
put your hand on my shoulder-
Showing Your perfect love on display-

I hear You speak in a gentle whisper,
"Relax and take a breath right here."
I feel You drawing near,
comforting me, making things clear.

Now I can finally hear You.
While I'm still and silent.
Nothing I can do,
but to sit and be quiet.

I wait excitedly and expectantly-
with ears open intently listening-
desiring for You to talk with me-
yearning for Your voice to speak.

This is the conversation I want.
When I am quiet and still.
Your voice has begun-
whispering wisdom and Your will.

So let's talk, and that means-
You do the talking, I'll be here-
listening to all You are speaking.

Read:

- John 10:27
- Psalm 62:5

Have you ever found yourself doing all the talking when you have a conversation with God?

_____

_____

_____

_____

_____

_____

How can you listen more when you are talking with God?

_____

_____

_____

_____

_____

_____

_____

Water That Spiritual Grass

We were in water restrictions stage two,
the yard got watered one day a week,
the grass dried up and turned brown too,
all from a lack of sufficient watering.

Are you watering your spirit?
Reading the Bible and praying.
Listening for God's voice ready to hear it.
Waiting, hearing what He is saying.

If you don't water your own grass,
the other side of the fence might look greener.
Don't believe that lie the enemy has,
mind your own yard, don't worry about your neighbor.

Avoid the spiritual drought,
now is the time to start the task,
there's plenty of water to go around,
go on and water your spiritual grass.

Read:

- Psalm 23:1-3
- Jeremiah 31:25

Do you water your spiritual grass? What prevents you from doing this? Are you too busy? Don't know where to start?

_____

_____

_____

_____

_____

_____

Write out a few steps you plan to take to avoid letting water restrictions affect your soul while going through this book. Some ideas might be:

- Journaling what you learn
- Listening to worship music
- Join a small group

_____

_____

_____

_____

_____

Transformation Help

Inside my mind.
Filthy.
Dirty.
Cleaning required.

Can't do it on my own.
I concede.
Help Needed.
Make this mind whole.

Renovate.
Rejuvenate.
Regenerate.
Invigorate.

Make me new.
Like only You can do.
I want to be like You.

I'm forgiven.
Erase this sin.
Renew from within.
I'm ready to begin.

So I desire.
Transform this mind.
To be as You designed.

Read:

- Romans 12:2
- Ephesians 4:23

How is your mind? Are your thoughts pure?

_____

_____

_____

Do you need it to be transformed? What are you spending time doing that influences your mind? Social media? TV? Internet?

_____

_____

_____

_____

Pray and ask God to work in any areas that need to be transformed.

_____

_____

_____

_____

Lost, Found, Hugs

When our daughter was younger,
we went shopping in a store.
We had rules set before her,
to stay with us, we'd done this before.

So, we walked in the store that day,
not expecting what came our way.

We were walking in the clothing section,
just shopping away, enjoying our time.
Then we took an unexpected direction,
Hannah was gone, outta our sight.

Heart pounds.
Hannah's not around.
Looking about.
Nowhere to be found.

We searched all over the place,
looking for our lost child.
Longing to see her little face,
we looked where we thought she might hide.

After looking through the section over again,
we went to the front of the store.
They asked us where she might have been,
we told them where we were before.

Then we heard her name said aloud,
the whole store was now aware.
Hannah was lost and needed to be found,
we were in shock, worry, and bit of despair.

Then we saw.
Now in Awe.
No longer distraught.
Hugging a lot.

We did not make her feel shame,
or bring up the rules we had set.
We made sure she was feeling safe,
and then hugged her neck.

That's how Jesus is when we run to Him,
He does not hold us off at arm's length.
He reminds us that we are forgiven,
and hugs us in His loving strength.

Read:

- Luke 15:20-24
- Hebrews 11:6

Have you ever felt like you couldn't go to Jesus because of sin or shame in your life? When?

_____

_____

_____

_____

Does it make a difference knowing Jesus just wants you to come to Him? There is no condemnation where He is. He is ready to hug you with His wide open and loving arms. Write out a prayer accepting Jesus' love for you. Describe how this feels and the impact it might have on how you can share this love with others

_____

_____

_____

_____

_____

_____

_____

_____

_____

_____

_____

_____

_____

_____

_____

_____

_____

Walking With A Humble Heart

God does not desire,
the strongest or the smart.
He loves the kind,
and humble of heart.

Think of others more than ourselves,
putting them first in life.
Do not brag about possessions or wealth,
instead help those in need and strife.

We dare not think ourselves as more,
than those we meet.
Let's always be willing to help the poor,
and those on the street.

When we come to the throne of grace,
bowing low, with a right heart.
We know His presence is in this place,
if we enter with the right attitude from the start.

Knowing that He lifts up the low,
and gives grace no matter the pain and scars.
All our needs He will provide
to those who know, to walk with a humble heart.

Read:

- Micah 6:8
- James 4:6-10
- Psalm 25:9
- 1 Peter 5:6

At what times or situations do you feel you might need to humble yourself to God?

_____

_____

_____

_____

_____

_____

_____

_____

What might that look like for you?

_____

_____

_____

_____

_____

_____

_____

_____

Praise Raised High

It is apparent to me that I don't worship the same
as others that are claiming to praise Your name
so I am wondering...

If I do not raise my hands or dance in a certain way-
does it mean I missed the plan for lifting up Your praise,
does it matter if I sit or stand?

In my heart I give You worth, You take first place
Should I be disturbed by how I lift my praise,
or just keep putting You first?

I'm just gonna praise the way that honors You
by lifting Your name not bothered by how others do,
I'm praising You my way.

You know my heart and how I glorify
at the start of morning and night,
my praises won't stop.

In my unique way I'll try to keep on going
lifting this voice of mine and showing
my praise raised high.

Read:

- Psalm 71:8
- Psalm 99:5
- John 4:24

Does your praise look the way others praise?

_____

_____

_____

_____

How do you worship? Singing? Dancing? Reading?

_____

_____

_____

_____

_____

Do you worship with a pure heart? What makes this
hard to do at times? How do you overcome it?

_____

_____

_____

_____

_____

_____

Beyond My Limitations

There are times when I let my limits,
define how much I can be used.
I'm not the best or the one that fits,
the area You have already approved.

I feel so inadequate at times,
You are so big and see it all.
I'll just sit here in my little life,
and know I'm limited and small.

I'm not good at talking to people,
or sharing my life's story.
I get nervous, words become unspeakable,
I would just make a mess of Your glory.

But then I am reminded,
of those You used in the past.
Their limitations did not define,
their usefulness in Your plans.

Moses did not want to speak,
but he led the captives free.

Paul had a bothersome thorn,
but Your grace was more.

Jonah ran and hid,
You caught him in a fish.

Matthew was a tax collector,
he became a disciple maker.

As I look through Your Word,
others were used even with their hesitation.
I will follow You, shining Your light to the world,
for You can move beyond my limitations.

Read:

- Exodus 4:1-10
- 2 Corinthians 12: 7-10
- Jonah 2:1-10
- Matthew 9:9-11

What limitations do you put on yourself?

_____

_____

_____

What lies are you believing about why God cannot use you for His purpose?

_____

_____

_____

_____

Write out a short prayer thanking God that He is greater than your self-perceived limitations.

_____

_____

_____

_____

_____

_____

_____

_____

_____

_____

_____

_____

_____

_____

_____

_____

_____

_____

_____

Spirit Breakout

Holy Spirit.
In me.
Breakout.
For all to see!

No permission is needed,
just flow right out.
Use this imperfect body,
to show what You're about.

Holy Spirit.
In me.
Breakout.
Let it be!

Let others see only You,
that is my desire.
Shown in all I say and do,
burning with that Holy fire.

Holy Spirit.
Burning.
Breakout.
Daily!

No holding back now,
breakout and show Your power.
show the world what You're about,
anticipating a supernatural encounter.

Holy Spirit. Breakout!

Read:

- 2 Timothy 1:7
- Romans 8:15
- 1 Thessalonians 5:19

Have you allowed the Holy Spirit to breakout in your life? What does/would that look like?

_____

_____

_____

_____

_____

_____

_____

_____

_____

_____

_____

_____

_____

_____

_____

There's Power In The Word

There is a book still today
that wields supernatural power-
It speaks in a powerful way
with words that last forever

This is God's own Word written down
lasting through all eternity-
No other word with this power can be found
no matter how far or wide you seek

There is no way to describe
the strength contained in it-
The words show the great might
of God's own Holy Spirit

Don't box up what it says
or limit the strength that's there-
this book raises the dead
from a place of hopeless despair

Hearts as hard as stone
are made soft like clay-
Unfamiliar paths are made known
with a light to show the way

Broken lives are made whole
bringing hope and joy-
Sin brought to the light and exposed
bringing relationships out of a deep void

The power is there for us to receive
if we will read and apply-
Turn the pages and just believe
be filled with the power that it supplies

Apply what you can learn
studying these pages-
There is power in the Word
to overcome challenges each day.

Read:

- Hebrews 4:12
- Psalm 119:11
- Psalm 33:6

**How do you experience the power of God's word?
Journaling? Meditating? Singing? Memorizing?**

_____

_____

_____

_____

_____

_____

_____

_____

_____

_____

Do you practice memorizing scripture? Why or why not? What power is there?

_____

_____

_____

_____

_____

_____

_____

_____

Share about a time when a verse gave you power.

_____

_____

_____

_____

_____

_____

_____

_____

_____

_____

_____

Four Acts For Saving The World

INTRO

Without Your work here,
there would be no hope.
You made the way clear,
the path to the Father known.

God's love for us on display,
His redemptive work is done.
These four acts show the way,
to salvation for each one.

ACT ONE

Jesus came to earth, just like us

He was God incarnate, but this was miraculous

The virgin now pregnant, and showing a baby bump

Some thought it's impossible, or maybe even disastrous

The Savior of the world, was to soon come

In this divine birth, He entered the world flawless

ACT TWO

Jesus lived among the people of His day-
Showing them how to live, the example on display

He loved everyone in the perfect love He has-
Showing that differences are all in His plan

He grew up, made friends, and went to parties-
Experiencing all these things without compromising

He experienced human needs, He got tired and slept-
Emotions were there, He laughed, He loved, and He wept

When temptation came, He resisted it with the Word-
His righteousness clearly shown, never blurred

He was wrongfully accused in the court-
And yet still, He did not make an inappropriate retort

Forced to carry His cross on His bloodied back,
He trudged up the hill to be crucified and stabbed

ACT THREE

Jesus' hands and feet nailed to a tree-
blood running down His body.
This sacrifice made for you and me-

The cross stood up for all to see-
dropped into its permanent place.
Set upon Mount Calvary-

The pain beginning to intensify now-
You could have called in help at any time.
Instead You stayed the course laid out-

And when there could be no more to take-
a spear is shoved deep in your side.
The full price for my sin was being paid-

Hanging by ankles and wrists-
pushing up to get a breath.
One final push, and it is finished-

With that final cry
He took His last breath.
The King had died.

ACT FOUR

The body taken off the cross
and put into a borrowed grave.
Carefully wrapped in burial cloths
laid to rest, but for only three days.

On that third day in the ground
Jesus walked out, risen alive.
No part of death could hold Him down
completing the work for eternal life.

Friends looked in the tomb
but He wasn't found there inside.
The work that was set out for Him
was now completed for all mankind.

There is now a complete redemption
all through God's perfect design unfolded.
His birth, life, death, and resurrection
show how He saved the world.

Read:

- Matthew 1:18-25
- John 1:14
- Luke 23:44-46
- John 20:1-9

Do you believe Jesus was born, lived, died, and rose again?

_____

Have you trusted Him for forgiveness of your sins?

_____

Take a few minutes and meditate on the magnitude of what Christ did for you. What came to your mind?

_____

_____

_____

_____

_____

_____

_____

_____

Ya, That's Forgiven

Sayin a whole lotta,
talk that's deceivin'-
using all that gossip,
ya, that's forgiven.

Mind all over the place,
not watchin what you're thinkin'-
thoughts full of hate,
ya, that's forgiven.

Reachin' up feelin bad,
forgiveness desired, now repentin'-
grace is here to be had,
because you're forgiven.

Gone back to your old ways,
stubborn, not listenin'-
hear what He says,
your old ways are forgiven.

Just turn around,
a different livin'-
His mercy is found,
because you're forgiven.

Read:

- Isaiah 1:18
- Acts 3:19
- Isaiah 44:22

God forgives all of our sins if we repent. What does it meant to repent?

_____

_____

_____

_____

Do you ever have difficulty repenting? Why?

_____

_____

_____

_____

Do you find it difficult to believe that God forgives us over and over? Why?

_____

_____

_____

Your Past Experiences Do Not Define Your Current Relationship

Sitting in church one day.
Listening to what the pastor says.

Then he switched it up.
Gave a task to us.

'Listen to the Lord speak, hear the Spirit.
See what He would say to you for a minute.'

Why would God speak to me?
I have done bad things recently.

Was it possible to even expect,
God to talk to me when I'm so imperfect?

I was not sure I would hear a word.
But, I sat that there, listening... then I heard....

It wasn't a loud voice,
but I heard it through all my inner noise.

"Your past sins do not define,
this relationship of yours and Mine."

I exhaled in relief,
hearing even through my unbelief.

What ever my past sin is,
it doesn't define my current relationship.

Read:

- Romans 8:1
- John 16:13
- 2 Corinthians 5:17

Take a minute and meditate on the fact that your past sins do not define your current relationship with God. What is God saying to you?

_____

_____

_____

_____

_____

What does God say to you about your relationship with Him?

_____

_____

_____

_____

_____

_____

_____

Break This Old Ground

I am set in my ways, I let nothing through
I like my routine; I hesitate when I see something new

Drama free is what I desire, let me be alone
this is the foundation I have laid; it is what I have known

It is easier this way and makes the most sense
I don't get hurt because of this great defense

This dry ground is serving me well today
keeping it clumped together like dried clay

Then You ask me if this is really what is supposed to be
and show me some of the finer things I am missing

I fight back standing on this old ground again
staying in my comfort zone in which I am livin'

Then You reach down and pull me up to you
touching the depths of my heart, trying to get through

You barely touch this old ground, and it begins to shake
the luxury of this old foundation begins to quake

I ask "Why" looking directly into Your radiant face
I like this secure and peaceful place

You answer with a calm whisper to the unreachable
and You tell me a part of the plan, and then abruptly stop

Saying get rid of this old ground if I want to see the rest
promising the way ahead is certainly the best

It is with great reluctance and fear deep within
I start to trust Your word and allow the breaking to begin

It is unstable for a while, and things rock back and forth
the place I once relied on is shaking me to the core

I know it's worth it and leads to a better place all around
so go ahead and tear it up, break this old ground.

Read:

- Luke 6:48-49
- Psalm 104:5

Which lines stand out the most to you?

_____

_____

_____

_____

_____

_____

_____

_____

What is it about those lines that caught your attention?

_____

_____

_____

_____

_____

_____

_____

Are there any old clay grounds you need to break down to receive God's best for you? What are they? Ask God to help you do this.

_____

_____

_____

_____

_____

_____

_____

_____

_____

Why Do I Ask

When I pray I ask for many things.
Some for other people some for me.

But what is my motivation?
What are my intentions?

Is it for more money?
Maybe more notoriety.

Am I praying for my enemy?
Or am I just praying selfishly?

How about praying for God's will.
And then listening and being still.

Certainly, God knows my heart already.
So, I lift up those requests daily.

But why do I ask God for this stuff?
Isn't what I have enough?

When I pray and my heart is right,
what difference does that make in life?

There is freedom to come to His throne.
I can do this in a group or on my own.

I definitely should do this.
With a heart that is chasing His.

So I take an appropriate stance,
I make my request known in every circumstance.

Keeping this in mind as I ask,
that Jesus be revealed at every glance.

Read:

- Philippians 4:6
- James 4:3
- John 15:7

What are your motivations for praying and making your requests known to God?

_____

_____

_____

_____

_____

_____

_____

_____

_____

_____

Do you ever ask God for things with selfish intentions? When? Why?

_____

_____

_____

_____

_____

_____

_____

_____

How do you balance knowing God already knows your heart, He wants you to ask Him, and asking with a right heart?

_____

_____

_____

_____

_____

_____

_____

_____

A Whole Lotta Wisdom

So many things
I could request-
what I really need
more than the rest...

wisdom

Money is not it
riches go fast-
only this is worth it
it's all that will last.

wisdom

When I don't know
don't have a clue-
which way to go
I'll just ask You.

send it

Send a whole lotta
this one thing-
Your knowledge
is what I need

wisdom

I'm asking freely
just as You said-
waiting expectantly
for Your Wisdom.

Read:

- James 1:5
- Proverbs 2:6
- Proverbs 3:13

Do you consistently ask God for wisdom?
Why or why not?

_____

_____

_____

_____

_____

_____

What kind of difference does it make knowing God
gives wisdom to those who ask?

_____

_____

_____

_____

_____

_____

_____

The Wide Road Looks So Much Better

Walking this road of life
it's a worn and uneven path
sometimes I wander off the side

This is a narrow way
it's not always easy
here I am trying to obey

I hear You say, "Stay on the narrow road
it leads to life and joy.
Don't stray down places you don't know
it's just a dangerous ploy."

I retort with pride in my mind,
"The road looks safe to me.
It's a wide path and I can find
the way where I'm supposed to be."

Then you hold my hand,
in Your gentle grasp.
"Trust Me, on that road it's hard to stand-
and the pretty view you see doesn't last."

I take another look in a long gaze
trying to see around all the bends
still thinking the best is my way.

I look over to Him and see His grin-
Again, half asking and half telling I begin,

"Are You sure about this? I think I see a smoother path,
and I'm fairly sure it's wider and troubles can be passed."

I notice the smile never leaves His face,
He walks me over to the fork in the road-
stops with His arm around my shoulder at this place.

He grabs me tight and looks towards the path that's wide,
rubs His beard with His hand and says, "You don't know,
and can't see, the pitfalls and traps on that road that hide;
there are places there that steal, kill, and destroy."

He points to the narrow road and says, "See this way?"
I look down a narrow trail with rocks and sticks.
"Yes, I see the narrow path that looks hard to take."

Still smiling, He keeps His gaze ahead,
"The wide road is not the one to travel.
Go down the path I will walk with you instead."

Fighting inside; wrestling thoughts in my mind-
I'm torn with knowing what's right;
but wanting to take the easy way out,
and trying my way, even with this doubt.

"What's so much better on the narrow road I see?"
I ask as I look again to the wide easy way right there.
Still pointing to the narrow part, He begins to speak,
"Just because a path looks simple, doesn't mean it's clear."

I ponder the thought for a second, then I hear-
"See this narrow road, right here?
I have traveled that way -- now hear me say,
this is the road you will want to take."

Yet here I am, and here at this fork I stand
trying to process all the words I heard
and undo my stubbornness as best I can

He continues to encourage me,
"Don't worry about what's around the bend.
You just watch the light I give for you to see.
Let Me guide you in this narrow path you'll be traveling.'"

In a small bit of shame, I look down.
Knowing that's the best way to go.
I feel His eyes look on me now.

"Don't fret, I'm always here for you,
just walk the narrow road,
and I'll keep you safe and secure."

So even though the wide road looks so much better,
I take a step down the narrow one instead.
I walk with Him by my side forever,
comforted knowing He is my protector and friend.

Read:

- Matthew 7:13-14
- Psalm 119:105

What times in your life were you tempted to go down the wide road? What happened?

_____

_____

_____

_____

_____

_____

_____

_____

What makes it hard to follow Jesus down the narrow road?

_____

_____

_____

_____

_____

God, Can I...

I had a conversation with God the other day,
it kinda went this sorta way...

Me: God, can I just do what I want?
        I think I know what should be done.

God: Sure. I'm here.
        Always near.

Me: Really?
        Seriously?

God: Yep. Sure can.
        I'm here if you need a hand.

I was all excited and ready to go,
I paused, deciding what to do first,
then I heard a voice whisper really low...

God: Hey. You sure?
        Going after your own pleasure?

Me: Yep, I can handle it.
        I got this.

God: You ready to take responsibility?
        For doin' your own thing.

Me: Wait, what?
        No.
        Never mind. I'll just do what You want.

Read:

- Luke 14:28
- Proverbs 16:1-3

Have you ever had a conversation with God like this?

_____

_____

_____

_____

Do you try to convince God that you know the way?

_____

_____

_____

_____

How do these verses remind you to ask God
for direction?

_____

_____

_____

_____

_____

Worry? Who Me?

I'm livin'.
I've got this.
I can handle it.
Then worry comes in.

Wait... Worry?
Who me?

I am confident and in control.
I have my path set out before me.
Because that is how I roll.
There is no need to worry.

The unexpected comes.
The undesired outcome arrives.
Then I start to worry some.
Trying to control my life.

I look up and ask why.
This is not my plan.
So, I decide.
To try and understand.

Then... You.
Give me a new view.

Worry gets me nowhere.
Well, maybe a sense of confusion.
It's not that I don't care.
But You give me a new conclusion.

Give it to You, the best planner.
I can't add a day to my life anyway.
I turn this worry over to the Master.
Residing in His love I stay.

Worry? Who me?
Not anymore.
I found the cure.
Worry has no more hold on me.

Read:

- Matthew 6:27
- Luke 12:22-34

In what situations are you most likely to start worrying (if any)?

_____

_____

_____

_____

_____

_____

_____

_____

_____

What makes it easy (or not) to turn your worry
over to God?

_____

_____

_____

_____

_____

_____

Write out a short prayer that you can use in times
of worry releasing the concern to God.

_____

_____

_____

_____

_____

_____

_____

_____

_____

The Refuge Maker

There is a place-
where we can take-
shelter from the pain-
and make it through the day.

He is the refuge maker,
the pain and sorrow taker,
the soul and spirit anchor,
the firm foundation layer.

This is a place of safety-
already created-
there for the taking-
available daily.

This is a shelter made just for you,
a place to rest, be restored and renewed.
No matter what you've been through,
come, be refreshed in His refuge.

Read:

- Psalm 62:8
- Psalm 91:4
- Proverbs 18:10
- Psalm 34:7-9

At what times do you feel you need this refuge?

_____

_____

_____

What prevents you from going to the refuge
God provides?

_____

_____

_____

Take a minute and rest in God's refuge place He has for
you. Listen for His voice. Write out what you hear Him
saying to you.

_____

_____

_____

_____

_____

Stop Looking So Hard

Looking all around.
Hoping Jesus can be found.
Focusing. Listening for any sound.

Scanning to my right.
Desiring to catch a sight.
Observing. Seeking with all my might.

Then I heard a voice.
Whispering with quiet joy.
Speaking. Cutting through the noise.

I stopped all I was doing.
Sat still and stopped moving.
Meditating. That voice pursuing.

That's when I heard.
'Hey you, I'm always near.
Stop looking so hard, I'm right here.'

'Listen with your heart.
That's the place to start.'
Saying. 'Stop looking so hard.'

Read:

- 1 Chronicles 16:11
- Jeremiah 29:13
- Acts 17:27

How hard, or easy, is it for you to sit and listen? Do you feel Jesus is near when you do this?

_____

_____

_____

_____

Do you find yourself feeling like you have to "do something" to be near Jesus? Why do you think that is?

_____

_____

_____

_____

Take a second and realize Jesus is close. What do you hear Him telling you?

_____

_____

_____

Walk and Listen

Doin' my morning walk
Me 'n Jesus doing our talk
Then I hear Him say,
"Try something My way."

One word.
He said, "Listen,"
Then I heard,
"It's a discipline."

I stopped talking.
Walking. Listening.

Air conditioners are running.
Crickets are buzzing.

What's the point?
My confusion voiced.

Then I heard Him say,
"Enjoy the sounds at play."

I continued my walk, silent.
Listening with intent.
New sounds I heard.
Sounds that never before mattered.

Sprinklers running.
Sometimes...silence...nothing.
Then a low rumbling.
Deer watching... then running.

I learned that from now on,
to get with Jesus the closest-
is not about all the talk,
but seizing the moment.

This time is really about,
practicing this new discipline.
It was today I found out,
In order to hear, I have to listen.

Read:

- Psalm 119:10
- Psalm 25:4-5

Have you ever considered listening to be a discipline?

_____

_____

_____

_____

Commit to taking a few moments each day during this devotional to listen for Jesus' voice. Write out your commitment here.

_____

_____

_____

_____

What distractions do you need to remove to just listen?

_____

_____

_____

_____

_____

_____

_____

_____

How can this new idea impact your quiet time?

_____

_____

_____

_____

_____

_____

_____

_____

_____

_____

Unbelievable Things

Look around!
Be astonished!
See what's going down!
God's not finished!

There are extraordinary things to come,
if He told us we would never believe.
God is still working, He's not done,
look around, notice, look and see.

It's amazing!
Wonderful!
Things are happening!
Incredible!

Maybe it is healing from sickness or pain,
perhaps a family member gets saved.

Sometimes it's a small victory,
or an awesome experience-
like seeing God's perfect glory.

Eyes open!
Observe!
Be expectin'!
Miracle!

Don't wait, you'll miss out,
watch for what God is doing.
See what He is all about,
He's undoing, renewing, and pursuing.

Take watch,
God is busy.
He's got,
unbelievable things.

Read:

- Habakkuk 1:5
- Isaiah 43:19

Do you ever stop and notice all the new and wonderful things God is doing around you?

_____

_____

Take a few seconds to reflect on just a couple of things God has done for you in the last week. What are they?

_____

_____

_____

_____

_____

Write out a short prayer thanking God for these. Ask God to help you see the wonderful acts He does in the coming days and weeks.

_____

_____

_____

_____

_____

_____

_____

_____

_____

_____

_____

_____

_____

_____

_____

_____

_____

_____

_____

Becoming What You Want Me To Be

Every day,
every way,
all I say,
in all I pray.

I'm becoming more and more,
what You want me to be-
You know what the future has in store,
it is done by Your perfect directing.

In all I do,
all I view,
all I've been through,
becoming like you.

Walking with me through hard times,
helping me be what You have planned-
all according to Your perfect design,
directing me by Your loving hand.

A ways to go,
but never alone,
I'm Your own,
fully known.

I count it a joy to be on this journey,
walking out this faith-
becoming all you want me to be,
following You in all Your ways.

Read:

- 1 Peter 1:15-16
- 2 Timothy 1:9
- 2 Corinthians 7:1

What part of your life needs to be changed so you can keep becoming what God wants you to be?

_____

_____

_____

_____

_____

_____

_____

_____

_____

Restoring Your Splendor

Sickness and pain come as a part of life,
and indeed, we make choices for sure-
paths taken lead to tough times,
but God can restore on us His splendor.

Like the prodigal son,
who ran off with his inheritance,
just to blow it all on some
fun and momentary happiness.

When the child came walking home,
his dad was not offended.
Instead, he gave him a ring and robe,
and restored the son's splendor.

The Israelites were sent into captivity,
because God's commands they ignored,
They were slaves for centuries,
but God's splendor on them too was restored.

Despite decisions made in the past,
return to God and remain in Him.
His love and care will last,
and God's splendor can be restored on you again.

Read:

- 1 Peter 5:10
- Hosea 6:1
- Psalm 103:1-5
- Psalm 23:3

Have you had times in life when God restored you?
When was this?

_____

_____

_____

_____

_____

Have you told anyone your restoration story? Write
out here what you might say to someone as a witness
to God's restoration power.

_____

_____

_____

_____

_____

Eyes Closed Listening

I'm trying to hear what You are saying-
asking for Your voice to scream in a whisper.
Sitting here, eyes closed, waiting-
patiently listening, I wait to hear.

The inner noises crash in on my mind-
I only hear my selfish thoughts now.
Wanting to quickly find-
a way to be quiet somehow.

I try to push the distractions out-
to concentrate on one voice.
Waiting for a whisper, a shout-
still surrounded by all the distracting noise.

There is a struggle of learning to focus-
discerning the sounds coming my way.
I'm desiring those words to show up-
listening for what You will say.

Hearing Your words is what I want most-
Your voice is what I am needing.
So here I am with eyes closed-
listening with my whole being.

Read:

- Luke 11:28
- Proverbs 1:33

What impedes you from hearing God?

_____

_____

_____

_____

_____

_____

What can you do to listen more effectively?

_____

_____

_____

_____

_____

_____

Called By My Name, Redeemed By Yours

You know my name
even though I have so much imperfection.
You understand my heart and remove my shame-
I am free under Your work of redemption-
all my sins completely forgiven every day.

You saved me
through Your redemptive work alone.
It was a long walk up to Calvary-
dying on a cross for sins to atone-
salvation work is done now offered freely.

Now the choice
to receive this gift that is offered.
A decision that cannot be avoided-
grab hold with praising words-
offering up this worshipping voice.

This truth endures
the work for which You came-
the reason my heart adores.
All because You called me by my name-
and I am redeemed by Yours

Read:

- Isaiah 43:1
- I Peter 2:21

How does it make you feel knowing Jesus calls you by name?

_____

_____

_____

_____

_____

_____

_____

How does accepting Christ's redemption affect your life?

_____

_____

_____

_____

_____

_____

_____

Make My Different Count

I am not the same as others You use.
Sometimes I am lame and I just flat out lose-
Drowning in my shame

This different gets in the way of the Master's plan.
There doesn't seem to be, a means to use this unique man-
Shame blocks what to see

I'm not like the others here, I make mistakes and look silly.
There is no use for me I fear, I am just built differently-
See as the plan comes near

I desire to be used by You, to show Your love, be a light.
Even if it is to just a few of those crossing in my sight-
Nearer now to what I can do

I want to be included, I don't want to be left out.
My different is made by You, I'll show what You're about-
Do Your work all the way through

Take what I have and make it work,
it doesn't have to be perfect or profound.
Let Your love be heard
and make my different count-
Through Your voice and Word

Read:

- Psalm 139:14
- Isaiah 64:8

Do you feel like your difference counts in the kingdom of God? Why or why not?

_____

_____

_____

_____

_____

How has God used your difference in the past?

_____

_____

_____

_____

_____

_____

_____

Divisions Be There Not

With all the pain in the world,
we should live in harmony.
Proclaiming to love Jesus,
and living in Christianity.

And yet, here we are still,
divided even amongst ourselves.
Deciding on carpet and paint color,
and size of entry way bookshelves.

This is how people looking in see,
the way we act toward each other.
Can you imagine the impact we could have,
if we would just love one another?

In our selfishness we rage on,
and we give in to immoral desires.
How much better would we be,
if we kept our mind on matters that are higher.

Let's come together as the church and the Church,
and all this fighting and bickering stop.
Show the light of Jesus to all,
and make all these divisions be there not.

Read:

- Romans 16:17-18
- 1 Corinthians 1:10-13
- Luke 11:17
- Psalm 133:1

Is there anything causing you to be at odds with other believers? Pray and ask God to reveal any divisions in your life. What did God reveal to you?

_____

_____

_____

_____

How can we (you) commit to stopping division among believers and the church?

_____

_____

_____

Write out a prayer of unity for your pastor(s) and church.

_____

_____

_____

_____

Quick To Forgive

Harboring wrong done to me,
feels justified where I'm at.
But, it is just a disease,
Jesus never did that.

Let's face it.
It's not forgive it.
Then forget it.
I'm gonna remember it.

The difference is a change of heart.
Letting go of those past wrongs.
Set the hurt feelings apart.
Freeing forgiveness is what belongs.

Since we are forgiven so much through Christ,
He provided the great example to follow.
Through His strength and might,
we can let the forgiveness freely flow.

It takes work.
It's not always easy.
It's an internal action word.
It's worth all the effort in forgiving.

I'm still working on this concept,
of being ready and willing.
I need to accept,
others have been forgiving.

So, let's be a people of grace,
and have that Christ-like willingness-
exhibiting to the world His face,
by being quick to show forgiveness.

Read:

- Matthew 6:15
- Colossians 3:13
- Proverbs 10:12

What does it mean to forgive others as Christ forgave us?

_____

_____

_____

_____

_____

What difference does it make knowing Christ forgave you?

_____

_____

_____

_____

_____

Is there any unforgiveness in your life?
Write out a short prayer forgiving others.

_____

_____

_____

_____

_____

_____

_____

_____

_____

_____

_____

_____

_____

_____

_____

_____

_____

_____

_____

Since God Loves The Whole World

God loved the whole world
Every woman, man, boy and girl

There is no difference to Him
He loves all - even the different

So, if He loves us all
Shouldn't we follow that call?

Love our neighbor
No matter the skin color

Treat all with respect
Without all the politics

Loving like He loves us
Living harmonious

Let's follow His training
Not societies failing

Love each other as we are
Locking together arm in arm.

Read:

- James 2:8
- Galatians 5:14
- John 3:16

How can you show God's love to your neighbor?

_____

_____

_____

_____

_____

_____

How does defining who your neighbor is affect the way you read this poem and these verses?

_____

_____

_____

_____

_____

_____

_____

_____

Me?

Who am I
that You would love?
I don't understand why
You care for this one.

So many are better
and smarter too.
They are worthier
of Your love and truth.

Yet You still choose
to adore me the same.
Even though You knew
all my sin and shame.

It is just me
You desire.
Loving and caring
only my heart required.

I'm giving You myself
it's all I have to offer.
Nothing have I withheld
it's just me You desire.

Read:

- 1 Corinthians 6:19-20
- Deuteronomy 6:5

Do you have times when you wonder how God could love you? What is it that causes you to think this?

_____

_____

_____

_____

_____

_____

_____

What in today's devotion helps you know Jesus loves you just the way you are?

_____

_____

_____

_____

_____

_____

_____

Called Into Service

Children?
Are you kiddin'?
What am I Missin'?
Not my decision!

And then, there I was at the children's desk,
serving, helping new kids get to their class.
I'm an introvert, talking to new folks is not my interest,
but when I'm called into service, no choice but to act.

It took me a while to get my service legs under me,
I was walking new folks around to rooms.
There's still apprehension and nervousness in serving,
learning what God has for me to do.

Are you being asked to serve?
Do you dodge the Spirit?
Twisting, running at every turn?
Slow down, listen, hear it.

It may not be with the younger kids,
you might get involved with the youth.
Maybe you could ask where you might fit,
and find somewhere to serve that's new.

There is great joy when serving where God wants you.
Take it from an introvert serving though I'm nervous.
Serving where you're called is the best act you can do,
so, listen to the Holy Spirit, you're called into service.

Read:

- 1 Peter 4:10
- John 12:26
- Deuteronomy 13:4
- Philippians 2:4

Where are you serving your church or community now?

_____

If you are not serving, do you feel God calling you to serve anywhere? Where might that be?

_____

_____

_____

_____

Take a minute and ask God to reveal to you any place He might be asking you to serve.

_____

_____

_____

_____

_____

_____

_____

It's All About Me, And It's All About You

You hung on the cross for all to see,
blood running, the only perfect sacrifice.
You did it all even if it was just for me,
it's all about You paying my price.

You knew my name the whole way,
and You suffered to cover my sin.
Fully aware of all my deeds and words I say,
You still walked the path of suffering.

The glory is Yours alone by design,
it was all You from the beginning.
It's all about You all the time,
reflecting You in the life I'm living.

This faith is all about You,
this salvation is all about me.
No matter what I say or do,
You took my sin all the way to Calvary.

You looked down through history,
all my sin and shame you knew.
This sacrifice was done just for me,
now I live my life to be all about you.

Read:

- 1 Peter 1:18-21
- Romans 5:8

What is the hardest concept to grasp presented here?

_____

_____

_____

_____

_____

_____

How do you respond knowing Jesus would die just for me and just for you?

_____

_____

_____

_____

_____

_____

Act Like I Believe It

There's a word I see—
Hypocrisy—
Yes that's me—
Yet, I believe.

One day,
it's one way,
then I change,
hypocrite is my name.

How is it I can say I trust You,
then turn around and do what I do?

It's opposite.
Not what I said.
I'm an idiot.
A hypocrite.

Do as I say—
not as I portray—
you make a change—
I'm stayin the same.

If I genuinely believe, I can't be a hypocrite,
I gotta live and act like I believe it.

Read:

- Romans 7:19
- Luke 6:46

When do you feel your actions don't match your words?

_____

_____

_____

_____

_____

_____

_____

Why do think this happens?

_____

_____

_____

_____

_____

_____

_____

_____

Let My Heart Break

I tend to get caught up in my own day,
not paying attention to those around me.
I pass by people not hearing a word they say,
it's not that I'm ignoring them purposefully.

Am I just so involved in my own life,
that I fail to see the pain of others?
Is it that the people full of strife,
are not on my mind, with not even a bother?

Help me to see others the way You do.
Let my heart see their pain.
Bring them to my attention too.
So I can notice them in Your special way.

Keep me from my self-centeredness.
I want to see them from Your eyes.
Let others catch my wandering senses.
Let my heart break for those down in life.

Some of these need Your strength and love.
They are alone and maybe hurting.
I'll be a conduit for Your affection from above.
As my heart breaks for those that are lonely.

Read:

- James 1:27
- Proverbs 19:17

Are there people in your life that need Jesus' love?
Do they see it from you?

_____

_____

_____

Does your heart break for the people like Jesus' heart
did? What causes hesitation in allowing yourself to
feel this?

_____

_____

_____

Ask God to include you in encouraging others. Pray
and ask God to bring a person (or persons) name to you
that might need encouragement. Now ask God for the
opportunity to be included in that encouragement.

_____

_____

_____

_____

I Want Those Glasses

Brand new glasses on my face
seeing clearer now than ever before-
noticing things I didn't yesterday
now able to see what's in store.

I want those glasses
to be able to see You-
I don't want to take any chances
of missing what You want me to do.

Give me clear sight
like those new glasses I had-
so I can know what's right
following Your perfect plan.

Read:

- Psalm 146:8
- Ephesians 1:18
- Psalm 119:18

Do you ever feel you have old, scratched up glasses when you are trying to discern God's will? Why do you think this is?

_____

_____

_____

_____

What causes you not to "see" God in your life?

_____

_____

_____

_____

_____

_____

_____

_____

_____

How can you "get new glasses" for seeing God working in your life?

_____

_____

_____

_____

_____

_____

_____

_____

_____

Sin, You Can Just Go Away

Sin.
You're not allowed.
I resist.
You're now bound.

Defeated.
You've no power.
I'm redeemed.
You get outta here.

Saved.
By Jesus' blood.
Claimed.
I am His beloved.

Go.
Depart today.
I know.
You must go away.

Read:

- Ephesians 6:11
- 1 Peter 5:9

What encouragement is it to know that we have the power to resist sin and temptation when it comes?

_____

_____

_____

_____

_____

_____

Has the knowledge that when we resist the devil he flees from us resonated with you? How can you make this more real in your life today?

_____

_____

_____

_____

_____

Frustration Rushes In

In rushes this frustration.
No relaxation.
Irritation overflows.
This annoyance grows.

Simple things.
Become complicated.
My mood swings.
Anger to now indifferent.

Leave me alone.
I'll stay home.
No people please.
That is much easier.

Then I get my attitude adjustment.
Stop making rash judgments.

Turn to God, let Him work.
He's in control, it's His world.

God gives wisdom freely.
Just ask when you are needing.

God can move the frustration mountain.
He will make a way you can count on.

Read:

- Isaiah 41:10
- Psalm 34:18
- Proverbs 29:11

Do you get easily frustrated and want to be alone? What causes this?

_____

_____

_____

_____

What actions or things frustrate you the most?

_____

_____

_____

How does the Biblical reading help you deal with or address frustration?

_____

_____

_____

_____

The Only Way To Know

Sometimes we get adversity,
and experiences that ain't our favorite.
Could it be that all these things,
are so we can help others through it?

So, it is here that I propose,
we go through things not for ourselves.
But, to know how to understand those,
that are suffering and need our help.

We can take our suffering and pain,
and turn it around for others' good.
Let's use our experience for their gain,
helping them stand where we've stood.

I am learning to rejoice in struggles,
knowing that everything can be used.
I'm grateful and can even chuckle,
knowing I might help others through a wound.

Come along with me as I'm thankful for this fun,
I turn this inconvenience into a way to help.
Knowing the comfort I might give has begun,
because I experienced these things myself.

Read:

- 2 Corinthians 1:3-6
- Roman 5:3-5

Are you prepared to comfort others? Ask God to give you wisdom in knowing when someone needs that comfort.

_____

_____

_____

_____

_____

_____

What experiences have you been through that make it so you can you be a comfort to others?

_____

_____

_____

_____

_____

_____

_____

Stuck In The Fog

Driving through the rolling hills-
the fog rolls in as the night brings its chills.

On the hilltop, I can see for miles-
down in the valley the fog resides.

Sometimes the valley seems to go on too long-
the fog of life seems like it will never be gone.

When will this valley road head back upward?
Hoping I'm going the right way, in the fog I wonder.

This haze blocks all light to my life-
I need help getting back my sight.

Slowly I can feel this cloud disappear-
climbing out of the valley to skies that are clear.

I'm once again able to see things now-
through that fog of life, I'm finally out.

Read:

- Isaiah 41:10
- Joshua 1:9
- James 1:2-3

Have you ever felt like there was a fog just hanging over your life? How would you describe the feeling?

_____

_____

_____

_____

_____

_____

_____

What comfort can we draw from these verses?

_____

_____

_____

_____

_____

_____

_____

My New Best Friend

I met a new friend today,
his name is Bell's Palsy.
He is here to stay,
a new companion for me.

He gives me lots of surprises,
and teaches me new things.
I get to cover one of my eyes,
and get to try new ways of drinking.

He doesn't keep me down,
I look on the bright side.
I know he'll always be around,
so together we'll have to reside.

No reason to be upset or wonder why,
God knows the purpose and the reason.
I'm just gonna embrace it and try,
to live out His purpose in this season.

So good ole Bell and I will be here for a while,
we will be here plugging away thinking of you.
So, remember this little poetic style,
in all your concerns God will see you through.

Read:

- Romans 5:3-5
- Psalm 41:3
- 2 Corinthians 4:17
- Romans 8:28

Do you have a concern, affliction, or worry you need to turn over to God? Write out your burden here and turn it over to God.

_____

_____

_____

_____

_____

_____

_____

_____

_____

_____

Renewed Well

I come to the renewing well
that is in Your presence.
I'm staying here until
I'm full in all my depths.

Feeling tired.
Needing renewal.
Here I've found.
Holy fuel.

When I'm depressed,
I bow right here-
Forgetting the rest,
I'm renewed by prayer.

Angry.
I hear a calming voice.
Changing.
You cause me to rejoice.

This renewal well is for all.
Accessible.
Get the to the well for renewal.
Available.

My mind is a mess,
a constant fight-
I need renewed to the fullest,
by Your might.

You are welcome to come and stay,
it's here He will indwell.
Refresh your mind and heart all the way,
here at this renewing well.

Read:

- Romans 12:2
- Isaiah 40:31
- Titus 3:5

When do you feel you need a renewing of your mind and soul?

_____

_____

_____

_____

_____

_____

_____

_____

In what ways are you renewed? Reading the Bible?
Worship? Fellowship?

_____

_____

_____

_____

_____

_____

_____

_____

How does being in the presence of Jesus help you get
renewed and filled?

_____

_____

_____

_____

_____

_____

_____

_____

Plugged Into Jesus

Walking through the airport
with coffee in hand-
waiting for the plane to board
watching people as they stand

They seemed to all gather
in one particular place-
seemed to be pretty popular
all up in each other's space

Looking around to see what's up
maybe there was something here-
there was a plain pole, except
it had electrical outlets front and rear

That's what it was I saw
people plugged into an invisible source-
power to laptops, iPads, and iPods
every outlet used in the concourse

Then the pondering hit
like a lead weight-
what if...just what if
we plugged in to Jesus that way

Do we let Him power our lives?
Do we plug in before the battery's dead?
What if we plugged in our 'hard drives'
and let Him power us instead?

The cool thing is, He's always there
we don't have to find a power outlet-
He will charge us up because He cares
we need no cables, no internet

Plug into Jesus today
and receive His power now
He will charge you up for the day
and give you strength as only He knows how

Read:

- Ephesians 6:10
- 1 Chronicles 16:11
- Psalm 105:4

Do you "plug in" to Jesus every day? Why or why not?

_____

_____

_____

_____

_____

_____

_____

_____

What prevents you from doing this?

_____

_____

_____

_____

_____

_____

_____

_____

_____

What can you do to start and/or maintain a habit of letting Jesus charge your energy for the day?

_____

_____

_____

_____

_____

_____

_____

_____

_____

Lion's Den Faith

Daniel was not scared to raise his hands,
and let his beliefs be known.
He worshipped his God in every land,
he never wavered under God's control.

He was told to bow down on a knee,
to the ruling king of the land.
Daniel did not give in to that decree,
he remained faithful, he took a stand.

He was captured but that didn't scare him,
they came and took him into custody.
Then he was thrown in the lion's den,
with another ultimatum to worship the wicked king.

Daniel didn't do it, he worshipped God,
even in the face of the lions there.
He kept his faith and remained strong,
God kept the lions from harming a hair.

That's how I want to live my life,
I want to be like Daniel.
Even when I get surrounded by strife,
and life feels like it's too much to handle.

I will not bow down to the current mood,
and give in to what the public says should be.
I will have a grateful attitude,
and I will not let the societal norm define me.

Just as Daniel did not bow down,
knowing what might lie ahead.
I will not bow to the pressures I've found,
even if it means I may face certain dread.

I will have this lion's den faith,
trusting God for everything.
Knowing He counted my days,
and has the best in mind for me.

Read:

- Daniel 6:16-23

At what times in your life have you felt like you were in the lion's den?

_____

_____

_____

_____

How did you get through this time?

_____

_____

_____

_____

_____

How does Daniel's example help you persevere when you might feel like you're in a lion's den?

_____

_____

_____

_____

_____

_____

Write out a plan to share a time when you had faith like Daniel.

_____

_____

_____

_____

_____

_____

_____

_____

_____

_____

Following All The Rules

I do my best to follow the rules,
I try to be better than when I began.
I do all that I think I need to do,
checking all the boxes I can.

Except.
Not Your requirement.
Relationships.
That's where it's at.

This journey is not about a set of do's and don'ts.
All that is required is a personal relationship.
It's not a matter of shouldn'ts, couldn'ts, and won'ts.
It's all about communication and togetherness.

This is such good news-
I've messed up a ton-
Broken almost all the rules-
And disobeyed some-

I'm so glad God does not require,
me to live a perfect life.
So, it's not about how hard I try,
my relationship with God is what I desire.

Read:

- Titus 3:5
- Jeremiah 24:7
- Hebrews 11:6

Have you been trying to live up to a rule or set of rules hoping to make God happy?

_____

_____

_____

_____

_____

How is it transforming to know that God wants a relationship with you, and that relationship is not about following a certain set of rules?

_____

_____

_____

_____

_____

_____

Lies Destroyed

There is a truth around,
that destroys all the lies.
Many lies may be found,
and they may be big in size.
The truth will abound,
and kill the lies as they arise.

Bitterness pops up like a weed after the rain.
I resent people and place on them all the blame.
But then Your truth resets my focus again.

You say, "Love them like I love you, my child.
That will destroy this life-draining lie."

Then I see a pretty image, it's stuck in my head.
The lust sneaks in, 'it's just a thought,' it said.
I turn and notice You on guard, ready to defend.

You whisper, "Don't be fooled by this voice."
So I resist the danger; this lie is now destroyed.

Jealousy comes riding in on a showy horse.
Reminding me that I think I always need more.
That's when I see You at my side, ready with force.

"Let's take this one on together," I hear You say.
Then jealousy is dismantled, no longer in my way.

I'm feeling at my best; pride comes storming in next.
I thought I was finished with all of these lies; I need rest.
Instead, residing within my heart, this one I try to deflect.

"Don't ignore this pride, turn it to gratitude and joy."
You remind me of this truth, so this lie can be destroyed.

I am comforted again and again,
by the sound of Your voice.
Sending me truth into which I can live,
making a way to discern all this noise.
Listening to You is how I begin,
ensuring all these lies are destroyed.

Read:

- 1 Corinthians 10:13
- James 4:7

What lies do you deal with regularly?

_____

_____

_____

_____

_____

_____

_____

_____

_____

What ideas or concepts presented here can help
you overcome the lies and deceptions?

_____

_____

_____

_____

_____

_____

_____

_____

_____

_____

_____

_____

_____

_____

_____

_____

_____

_____

It's A Death Sentence

My sin.
Your sin.
All within.
Where to begin.

It starts with a thought,
a quick second glance.
Mind wondering where it ought not,
gives temptation a second chance.

Death is near.
That voice is clear.
It begins here.
Now enters fear.

Perhaps it is a degrading word,
or gossip coming from the heart.
The mouth deals out pain and hurt,
giving inner desire another place to start.

Now a debt.
Death sentence.
Eternally set.
Mandatory recompense.

The result of all our sin is a horrible death,
this punishment has to be dealt out.
Payment is required for the eternal debt,
it must be paid in full somehow.

Jesus steps in.
Takes the punishment.
Clears my sin.
New life again.

Jesus took my sin, the death sentence I owed,
paid for it on the cross You carried up Calvary's hill.
It took Your death where blood and water flowed,
to cover my sin, bringing me back to a life You fill.

Debt paid.
Sin forgave.
Now saved.
Freedom today.

Read:

- Isaiah 53:5
- 1 Peter 2:24

What line or stanza stood out to you? What is it about those words that caught your attention?

_____

_____

_____

_____

_____

_____

_____

What spiritual concept hit you the most?

_____

_____

_____

_____

_____

_____

_____

_____

Write out a prayer of thanksgiving to Jesus for paying
your debt of sin.

_____

_____

_____

_____

_____

_____

_____

_____

_____

127

Pulling The Roots Of Sin

When weeds come up through the grass,
and start to take all the water and nutrients-
cutting off the leaves won't stop them from coming back.
the roots must be pulled to stop the weed from returnin'.

The same goes for sin in life,
the root must be killed below the dirt-
no matter how hard you try,
dig up the roots, or the sin will return.

If this means forgiveness is in need,
don't hesitate to ask for it-
maybe you need to forgive completely,
get it done, don't ignore it.

Bitterness has a really deep root,
takes a lot to dig it out-
don't let it reproduce,
even the smallest root will sprout.

No matter what root is there,
get rid of it as soon as possible-
dig it up with haste and care,
weed out the garden of your soul.

Read:

- Hebrews 12:15
- Mark 7:20-23

Is there a "root" in your life you need to dig up and get rid of today? What is it?

_____

_____

_____

_____

_____

What action step today (forgiveness, repentance, etc.) will you take?

_____

_____

_____

_____

_____

More Mercy

If I only knew
how much mercy
came from You.

It's not just there
every morning
but anytime anywhere.

Morning, noon, night
mercy shows up new
always there on time.

My wrongs covered
not getting
what I deserved.

Thank You
for more mercy
coming through.

Read:

- Lamentations 3:22-23
- Titus 3:5
- Ephesians 2:4-5

Define "mercy". What does it mean to you?

_____

_____

_____

_____

When have you experienced God's mercy the most?

_____

_____

_____

_____

How does it comfort you knowing God's mercy
is always there?

_____

_____

_____

_____

You Already Know

My thoughts and dreams
are an open book-
all my desires and needs
are already known by you.

I'm here to tell you all the things
it's what I'm supposed to do-
I know You're here listening.

I spill my guts, telling You
all my requests old and new.

You already know what I'm going to say.

You are not surprised by anything I'm prayin'
Sometimes I think I'm crazy.

But You always stay by my side
and listen to every word-
all that's in my heart and mind.

Even though You already know
You want to hear it anyway-
all the hurt, pain, and sorrow
and the requests for each day.

So here I am... telling You it all.

Read:

- Matthew 6:7-8
- Psalm 139: 2-4

God knows our desires and needs, yet He still wants to hear from us. Do you hold desires back from God when you pray? Why?

_____

_____

_____

_____

_____

God wants us to bring all our requests. Write out a short prayer of requests you may have not brought to Him before.

_____

_____

_____

_____

_____

_____

I Don't Want To

I reached up to my Daddy,
I had selfishness in my heart.
He reached down to me,
Pulled me up by my arms.

He asked me what was going on,
I saw love in His eyes.
How did Daddy know my thought?
Now I almost wanna cry.

I looked up at Him,
Still seeing that deep love-
I tried to speak again,
All my fears now undone.

I mentioned all the things
I know I'm supposed to do.
He looked at me intently,
I blurted out, "I don't want to!"

He smiled and gave his belly a rub.
"What is it you think is too much?"
Words running in my mind, I hesitated some,
trying to put thoughts together and such.

I finally spoke up, now unsure what to speak,
realizing what He had already done.
I sat up in His lap, He looked down to me,
still desiring to talk with Him some.

"People expect me to be good,
I'm not sure I want to all the time."
He squeezed me tight, like a dad could,
He whispered in my ear really light...

"If you know what is good, just try that.
You can't go wrong if it's the right thing to do.
I know it's hard to follow some commands,
and sometimes, you just don't want to."

Daddy knew exactly with what I was dealing.
Just His look gave strength and encouragement.
At least now I had a better attitude and feeling,
though still harboring a feeling of discontent.

Daddy knew my inner struggle right away,
gave me the encouragement to follow through.
So, it's the good road on which I'm trying to stay,
Even in the times when I don't want to.

Read:

- James 4:17
- 2 Corinthians 8:21

Do you ever find yourself not wanting to do the right thing?

_____

_____

_____

_____

Do you ever feel God offering to help? When?
How did/do you respond?

_____

_____

_____

_____

_____

_____

_____

_____

_____

_____

_____

_____

_____

_____

_____

_____

_____

_____

_____

Obedience Like Noah

I want to be just like Noah,
build this life out of obedience.
Even if I get made fun of,
I will still follow Your guidance.

When You say go,
make my obedience grow.

Just like Noah took Your plans,
and did not even flinch.
He built an ark with his hands,
obeying all Your directions.

When You say do it,
help my obstinate obedience.

Then Noah gathered the animals,
two-by-two just as You said.
Then the rain began to fall,
filled the earth til no land was left.

When You say get ready,
help me to just obey.

When people look at me and laugh,
or try to make fun of me.
They see me obey and they attack,
help me to still act obediently.

When I hear Your voice,
obedience is my only choice.

Read:

- Hebrews 11:7
- Genesis 6:13-22

Have you ever obeyed God and got ridiculed
or laughed at? What was the situation?

_____

_____

_____

_____

Have you ever been hesitant to obey because you
thought others wouldn't understand?

_____

_____

_____

_____

How did you feel knowing you obeyed God?

_____

_____

_____

_____

_____

Hurt Feet and Other Needs

When my daughter was littler,
probably around nine or ten years old-
her feet hurt in the shoes we had for her,
she didn't wear them no matter what she was told.

Maybe she needed shoes that were newer,
so off to the store we went to see what we could find-
come to find out, her feet were bigger,
and she needed a larger size not a different kind.

We felt bad for not knowing,
her feet had grown-
and her feet were hurting,
in the shoes she owned.

We have a heavenly Father,
who knows our every need-
even before we notice the hurt,
He is completely aware and ready.

Before our feet feel the pain,
when we don't understand our purpose-
He alone can show the way.
He is there to uplift us.

He is aware of all our situations,
and He can heal our pain-
give us direction in all our decisions,
God knows every problem we face.

Read:

- Philippians 4:19
- Luke 12:7
- Matthew 10:30-31

Do you ever feel like God doesn't know what you're going through, like we didn't realize our daughters feet had grown and now her shoes caused her pain?

_____

_____

How does it help knowing that God knows every part of you?

_____

_____

_____

_____

Tell God you realize He knows you, and you want Him to heal/comfort every part of you.

_____

_____

_____

_____

_____

Smothering Kindness

When Jesus saw the sinners,
He had great compassion.
In fact, He even became their defender,
so, we should act in His fashion.

We have no right to judge and hate,
we should smother people in kindness.
Not that sin should be tolerated,
but let's lift each other up in His design.

We are to love our neighbor,
as we love ourselves.
We should not be a gossip naysayer,
using people to get ahead.

When someone sins and confesses,
we should be the first to be kind.
Showing them how Jesus blesses,
and being of His ways and mind.

The moral of this story,
is for us to be like Jesus is.
To show the world a different way,
of smothering each other in kindness.

Read:

- Luke 10:27
- Colossians 3:12

What makes it hard for you to be kind to some people?

_____

_____

_____

_____

_____

_____

Write out a prayer committing yourself to showing kindness to those around you.

_____

_____

_____

_____

_____

_____

_____

_____

_____

Hi, Me Again

Well, it's me-
messed up.
again.
and again.
and again.
Back at Your feet-
longing to be forgiven.

I'll get it right one day-
following Your command-
learning to discern Your way-
led by Your guiding hand.

Hi, it's me. Yep, me.
I sinned.
again.
and again.
Seeing the empty cross and the grave-
You pardoned me by the life you gave.

I get back up to keep going steadily-
walking in Your steps-
my eyes on the road ahead of me-
letting go of all those regrets.

Hi, me again.
Sure did, did it again.
and again.
Still struggling doing things-
not the way I should be livin'.

Once again You look at me-
without the least bit of hesitation-
explain that all has been paid already-
and there is no condemnation.

So I stand here in Your presence-
not scared to say, it's me again-
knowing You love me without resentment-
and Your great joy over me calling Your name.

Read:

- *Psalm 130:3-4*
- *2 Chronicles 7:14*

Do you find it intimidating or scary to ask for forgiveness for the same sin over and over? Why?

_____

_____

_____

_____

How does His grace always covering your sin impact how you come to Him for forgiveness?

_____

_____

_____

_____

All This Mess

My life is a lot less
than a perfect example.
I've got all this mess
no one should follow.

It's not pretty
and there is some shame.
In fact it's ugly
and causes me pain.

All the times I didn't listen
resulting in disappointment.
Stubbornly doing my own thing
now requiring atonement.

I take this mess and lay it at Jesus' feet
knowing I'll find love and mercy.
Not looking back I leave
restored now into His will for me.

Leaving the mess I created behind
I start another day under grace.
Grateful this forgiveness is designed
to erase all my messy mistakes.

Read:

- Philippians 3:13-14
- Luke 9:62

Is it easy leaving your "mess" behind after taking it to Jesus? Why or why not?

_____

_____

_____

Are you holding onto parts of your mess rather than giv-ing it all to Him? What is it about those pieces you want to hang on to right now?

_____

_____

_____

Write out a prayer releasing any messes you are currently hanging on to.

_____

_____

_____

_____

_____

Plugged Ears Listening

Ears are plugged full of pressure-
all the voices around me sound weird.
I try to clear the ears so I can hear,
but the pressure just returns into my ear.

It takes extra effort just to listen,
to hear what people are saying.
Wonderin' what I might be missin',
because my ears are plugged today.

That's how I feel sometimes,
when I'm tryin' to be praying.
These plugged spiritual ears of mine,
can't seem to hear and are aching.

I plug my nose and try to pressurize,
these ears to get them to clear.
All that seems to do when I try,
is make the Spirit's voice disappear.

I wait for these plugged ears to hear,
all that You are saying to me.
Let them become free and clear,
so I can hear while I am listening.

Read:

- John 9:31
- Psalm 34:11

What do you think causes your spiritual ears to plug-when listening to God?

_____

_____

_____

_____

_____

_____

_____

How can you "clear your ears" to better hear Him?

_____

_____

_____

_____

_____

_____

_____

_____

Shattered Into Wholeness

I have fallen short, once more I've sinned,
I feel unworthy to approach the throne.
I tried my best but messed up again,
I can't seem to do this on my own.

I try to build up the courage to come,
and attempt to take a single step.
I see myself as broken and undone,
knowing my past, I fear what's next.

Fantasies that I have thought internally,
and the actions I took, and more.
Now, all these things that should not be,
crash in, and this life is shattered on the floor.

I hear a voice calling out to me,
saying all the wrongs can be forgiven.
Whispering to me that I can be healed,
all that is required is this next decision.

So, one reluctant foot in front of the other,
I hesitate, stop, then onward again I start.
I move closer to You, seeing I must go further,
to get to where I need to be, right where You are.

As I move closer, I feel myself start the inner destruction,
I power on with all my remaining boldness.
My spirit is shattered because of my imperfections,
yet You encourage me on, showing me Your wholeness.

Still, Your greeting breaks me into pieces,
I am not worthy to embrace Your forgiveness.
I pull back, felling myself trying to resist,
the nudging and calling to come into Your presence.

I push forward toward Your throne of grace,
broken, feeling the rest of me being shattered.
I know this is the perfect place,
to have all these pieces put back together.

I reach to Your hand stretched out my way,
giving You all these broken pieces that I hold.
This is the place I have longed to stay,
where You turn everything shattered into wholeness.

Read:

- Hebrews 4:16
- Psalm 30:2

**Do you ever feel shattered? How do you
overcome the feeling?**

_____

_____

_____

_____

_____

_____

_____

How does knowing Jesus accepts us as we are, even in a shattered state, help you long to be in His presence?

_____

_____

_____

_____

_____

_____

_____

_____

_____

_____

Write a short prayer expressing your desire to continually follow Jesus into wholeness.

_____

_____

_____

_____

_____

_____

_____

Clattering of Broken Dishes

Working in food service for a while,
learning to clean tables
and put plates in a pile.

Stacked up plates on a dolly,
moving them to the washing area
to be washed and cleaned.

Pushing the dolly way too fast,
stopping suddenly at the washer
everyone hears a big CRASH.

Noise so loud my ears hurt,
pieces of plates everywhere
no way to put them back together.

Does your life sound like those plates?
A big crashing sound that hurts ears,
with pieces shattered all over the place.

Or maybe your life has a little buzz,
that is irritating and annoying-
and causes others to run.

Take a listen to your life sound,
make sure there is no distracting noises-
so that you are one others want to be around.

Live a life that is pleasing,
resounding with a joyful noise-
loving people without ceasing.

Read:

- John 13:34-35
- Romans 12:18
- Galatians 5:14

Can you think of a time when your life might have sounded like a pile of plates crashing to the floor?

_____

_____

_____

_____

_____

_____

When have you observed an individual's life crashing but you did not hear the crashing plates sound? How did that person live so that there were not broken pieces all around despite the crashing circumstances?

_____

_____

_____

_____

_____

_____

_____

Lifted Out

When despair comes in rushing-
Depression is knocking on the door-
There is a hand that is reaching up-

All energy is gone, there is no more-
Dark clouds creep in overhead-
No reason to face all that's in store-

Not even trying, giving up instead-
What's the purpose of trying-
Going back to lay down in bed-

Then a voice calls out lightly-
"Let Me carry your burden"-
Emotions come, now starts the crying-

I sense this depression start to end-
Not knowing what this is about-
I feel the gentle call helping again-

Now I see above the dark and gloomy cloud-
Knowing He carried me up to where it's safe-
Finally, I am lifted out-

Read:

- Matthew 11:28-30
- Psalm 55:22
- Isaiah 41:10

How does it impact you knowing the Lord's ways are light and He helps us even when we may not feel it?

_____

_____

_____

_____

_____

_____

_____

_____

_____

_____

_____

_____

_____

I Stand Up Forgiven

I run.
falling-
I'm done.
guilty.

Looking up I see
Your eyes-
looking at me.
I cry.

Shame.
it lives inside-
Blame.
it's all mine.

You reach down.
Helping-
Touching me now-
Though I'm sinning.

Can't get up.
Sin is heavy-
Weight is too much.
I'm not ready.

Your touch-
lifts the burden.
A forgiveness rush-
I'm no longer hurting.

Get to my knees.
Weight is leavin'.
You lift me up.
I stand forgiven.

Read:

- 1 John 1:9
- Ephesians 1:7

Do you feel like you can stand forgiven?

_____

_____

_____

_____

What gets in the way of fully realizing this truth?

_____

_____

_____

_____

_____

_____

_____

_____

Don't Miss This Chance

When someone asks you
why you are happy.
Be prepared and ready to
respond truthfully.

A little button on my coat,
was all it took one time.
It said, "On the rock, and in the roll,"
displayed proudly on the outside.

Then a coworker asked in a group,
"What does that mean?"
The button was not a secret and I knew,
exactly what I believed.

I hesitated.
Words escaped.
Scared.
Unprepared.

I mumbled something like,
"It's rock and roll,"
Then the question came twice-
'What does it mean, I want to know.'

I was stunned, nothing to say,
I let the moment get away.

I replied with the same words as before.
Losing the chance to tell of my Savior.

The time will come when it's your turn,
and hopefully from this you can learn-
be prepared for when you are asked,
and don't miss this chance.

Read:

- 1 Peter 3:15
- Romans 10:10

Have you ever missed a chance to share Jesus like I did?

_____

Are you prepared to declare the reason for your joy?

_____

Consider having a family member or friend ask you
about your Jesus story. Practice what you will say so you
do not miss the chance that you get to share the love of
Jesus with others. Then, write out what your response
might be to someone who asks you about your faith.

_____

_____

_____

_____

_____

Blessed by Grace

If we look around at all we have,
the material things seem to add up.
We can't help but look about and laugh,
and realize we have so much stuff.

And yet, nothing we have compares
to what You give if we just accept it.
This gift is not justified or fair,
and yet so many reject it.

Nothing we own even comes close,
and there is no way to replace.
This is the greatest present known,
it is us being blessed by His grace.

We can't do anything to earn it,
still He gives it for free.
We do not deserve it,
it's free to all who believe.

This grace is better than the sleekest car,
shinier than the biggest diamond ring.
His grace is more valuable than the stock market,
it is the present we don't want to be missing.

Just what is this grace spoken about here?
I'm glad you asked, let me tell you.
It is a gift we cannot earn
yet, it's not getting what we do deserve.

It's not paying the price for our sin.
That has already been paid.
The only cost for us is to believe in Him.
And that is how we are blessed by grace.

Read:

- Ephesians 2:8-9
- Romans 5:1-5

Have you ever considered the blessing of God's grace? Why or why not?

_____

_____

_____

_____

_____

_____

What thoughts or feeling does that bring to mind?

_____

_____

_____

_____

_____

_____

Be Encouraging

I played bass guitar in the church worship band.
I really have no rhythm, but I did okay with what I had.

I got off beat, and sometimes played the wrong note.
My guitar friend looked over at me, shaking his head, no.

He never belittled me, or told me to give up,
he always helped me and encouraged me no matter what.

Be like my friend was every time,
even when the right note I couldn't find.

Be encouraging.
Not discouraging.

Stay inspiring.
Not degrading.

When friends hit a wrong note in life,
or have no rhythm due to stress or strife-
be encouraging to them in a special way,
you never know how much it's gonna make their day.

Read:

- 1 Thessalonians 5:11
- Ephesians 4:29

Are you intentional about encouraging people in your life?

_____

_____

_____

_____

_____

_____

_____

What steps can you take today to be more consistent about being encouraging?

_____

_____

_____

_____

_____

_____

Your Love

Wrap Your love around me-
let me feel it warm my inner being-

When I'm scared late at night-
I need Your love to make it all right-

I'm anxious for all there is to do today-
Your love is the only thing that makes it OK-

This love is my only desire-
It makes all my burdens lighter-

There is nothing without Your love-
Please send it down from up above.

This is Your love that abounds-
Covering me tight, all around.

Read:

- Psalm 119:76
- Psalm 30:5
- Psalm 31:16

Reflect on a situation in which you desired to feel the love of Jesus. What was that situation?

_____

_____

_____

_____

_____

_____

How did it feel when you knew He was there with you?

_____

_____

_____

_____

_____

_____

My Sister's Sheep

My sister lived on a small farm,
she had a llama, a cow, and some sheep.
She loved it even though it was hard,
giving all the animals food to eat.

I was there one time,
when she let the sheep out.
They scattered, then started to cry,
so, she would gather them with a shout.

They heard her voice and came,
right to her with confidence.
The sheep knew they were safe,
with her in the field, there were no threats.

Those sheep knew her voice alone,
I tried to call them to come to me.
It was only her voice they had known,
they moved when they heard her voice only.

Do you know Jesus' voice?
Have you wondered off on your own way?
Listen for Him to call through the noise.
Come to Him, He calls your name.

Read:

- Psalm 100:3
- Isaiah 53:6
- John 10:14

Do you know Jesus' voice when you hear it? How?

_____

_____

_____

_____

_____

_____

_____

Is it comforting to know that Jesus calls to us and we can know His voice? When do you hear His voice the most?

_____

_____

_____

_____

_____

_____

_____

Search For The Lost Diamond

The diamond fell out of my wife's wedding ring.
She searched all over the house for that thing.

She went around, searching room by room.
She even tore apart the nasty vacuum.

Opening up the vacuum cleaner,
she saw all the nasty dirt before her.

She searched through all the dirt and grime,
looking desperately for the diamond.

The diamond wasn't big or fancy,
but it was the one from her ring.

She continued digging through the muck,
not stopping until she looked through all the gunk.

She went through it all with a fine-tooth comb.
She found it! The diamond was home.

Do we search for Jesus just like that?
He is worth finding no matter where we are at.

Read:

- Psalm 27:8
- Isaiah 55:6
- Proverbs 8:17

Do you seek after Jesus like my wife looked for her diamond?

_____

_____

_____

_____

_____

How can you seek Jesus today?

_____

_____

_____

_____

_____

_____

_____

_____

Doubting (My Name Here)

Sometimes when I pray
I don't expect You to act-
There's a doubt I can't explain.

Can You pull me through?
Will it all be OK?
Am I just confused?

All the questions swirl in my mind
hoping, waiting to see what You can do-
looking for my own special sign.

Help me to not doubt
trusting all the time-
knowing You have me now.

Leaning on You for today
remembering You care about-
all of me in Your perfect way.

Read:

- James 1:6
- Proverbs 3:5-8
- Matthew 21:21

Do you have doubt when you pray?

_____

_____

What is it that causes us to doubt?

_____

_____

_____

_____

How do you overcome doubt?

_____

_____

_____

_____

_____

_____

_____

Four Ways Of Pressin' Through

When there's sickness in my life,
and despair starts to show.
I found these four ways might,
help get through life's lows.

First thing I do is call on prayer warriors,
get those prayers going strong.
This is the foundation need to carry ya,
through what life brings along.

Second of all, I worship,
I like the old-time hymns.
Sing how God is in control,
and give the rightful place to Him.

Maintaining a sense of humor,
is essential in trying times.
I know it's not easy here,
but it has helped me in life.

Fourth, and certainly important,
is to acknowledge God is in control.
He has surrounded you with a fortress,
and completely loves your soul.

By keeping these four things in mind,
it has helped keep me renewed.
There's comfort when we find,
four ways of pressin' on through.

Read:

- Galatians 6:2
- Psalm 63:7
- Isaiah 41:10

Have you made a list of prayer warriors you can call on in a time of need? Consider making a list, it may be easier than trying to remember these individual sin times of need.

_____

_____

_____

_____

_____

Do you have a worship playlist like on your phone or MP3? If not, consider having one and listening to it even when you are not having a rough time. Write out a few songs you might consider having on that play list.

_____

_____

_____

_____

_____

_____

What does it mean to you that God is in control and He loves your soul? How is that comforting to you in hard times?

_____

_____

_____

_____

_____

_____

_____

_____

_____

_____

_____

_____

_____

_____

_____

_____

_____

_____

_____

This Broken World

People getting sick-
Back pain-
Rich getting richer-
This world breaks.

Sin abounds-
Convictions compromised-
Love hardly found-
World in demise.

Bombs dropped-
Reasons unfair-
Innocent lives lost-
World full of despair.

Pain and heartache-
Relationships broken-
Family members being fake-
Cutting words spoken.

This broken world needs Your healing-
Come rescue this land-
make better all we're feeling-
by Your healing hand.

Read:

- Philippians 3:8-10
- John 16:33

Do you forget sometimes that Jesus has overcome the world? How does it help to remember He is the healer and redeemer of the world?

_____

_____

_____

_____

_____

_____

_____

_____

_____

_____

_____

Every Room But This One

I heard Him call my name one day.
"Hey Marshall, wanna let me in?"
I looked up, feeling the rising shame-
I knew exactly what He was sayin'.

There's this one little spot,
deep within my heart that's private-
I hide my sins there with a lock,
and keep it closed and hidden.

Now, Jesus was asking me to open the door,
and let Him in to see all this mess-
My junk filled the room from ceiling to floor,
no one had ever seen what I had assembled.

I heard a knock on my door again,
"Hello? Can I come in now?"
I could feel the internal judgement begin,
seeing all this stuff gathered around.

I cracked the door and looked in His eyes,
"You sure You want to see this junk?"
He smiled back at me and replied,
"Yep, I'm here to help clean this stuff."

"I don't know. How about any room but this one?"
I said hoping He would be satisfied with that.
"I've seen those rooms already my son,
they are good, it's this one I want to look at."

"It's awfully dirty in here," I replied.
"I know," He said not forcing Himself inside.
I saw Him smile at me as He gazed into my eyes.
"I'll be right here when you're ready my child."

I was in a dilemma, do I let Him in this room?
It was my private area I didn't want to reveal-
Perhaps He's seen it all and already knew,
was it just me being stubborn, needing to conceal?

Read:

- Psalm 26:2
- Proverbs 27:19
- Psalm 139:23

Do you have a "room" in your heart or life that you don't let Jesus in to clean up?

_____

_____

Do you ever hear Jesus knocking to come in that room?

_____

**What does that sound like to you? A loud knock?
A soft whisper?**

_____

_____

Will you let Him clean up those parts of your life today?

_____

_____

_____

Write out a sentence or two giving God permission to
clean out every room in your heart. Include a statement
of commitment to open the locked doors of these
rooms. What would that look like for you?

_____

_____

_____

_____

_____

_____

_____

_____

_____

_____

_____

_____

_____

Under Crashing Walls

We stand strong in our strength-
Feeling strong under our own private might-
There is no feeling of weakness or outlook of defeat-
Feeling good, everything is going right-

All of a sudden.
Everything changes.
Soon to be done in.
Destruction in range.

And the world comes undone-
Everyone is plotting against you-
This is no longer enjoyable and fun-
The walls of despair come crashing through-

Nowhere to go.
No strength left.
The winds blow.
Bringing walls deft.

There seems to be no way out-
Stuck, breathing hard, trapped with no air-
Anchored to the floor with the weighty bricks all about-
Soon to be crushed under the walls, you only have
prayer-

Now cry to God.
Your last breath to use.
He's all you got.
Let Him rescue.

He will remove every fallen wall-
You will be able to breathe again and stand-
The crushing weight of these emotions are made small-
The Lord will clear these walls with His mighty hand-

You're up again.
Ready to fight.
Let joy begin.
Feel the day light.

The feeling of being crushed has passed-
You are now able to rise up and face every day
God has cleared the crashing walls and opened the path-
Now there are no bricks from the old wall in your way.

Read:

- Isaiah 41:10
- Psalm 27-1-3

What stanza or line stood out the most to you?

_____

_____

_____

_____

_____

_____

What is it about that part that caught your attention?

_____

_____

_____

_____

_____

_____

_____

How do you remind yourself of the strength found
in Jesus?

_____

_____

_____

_____

_____

_____

_____

_____

_____

_____

He Is Not Dead

Denied.
Jeered.
Crucified.
Speared.

Bleeding.
Tortured.
Beaten.
Death ordered.

>Taken down.
>Place to lay.
>Grave found.
>Dead 3 days.

>Risen now.
>He's alive.
>Walking around.
>Saving lives.

>>Praise His name.
>>He's not dead.
>>No longer in a grave.
>>He's alive instead.

Read:

- Luke 24:1-6
- Romans 10:9
- Acts 4:33

Here's the question, do you believe Jesus died and rose again on the third day? If not, what is preventing you from believing? If so, have you shared that with anyone?

_____

_____

_____

Have you accepted this truth in your life?

_____

_____

_____

In what ways do you feel comfortable sharing this with others?

_____

_____

_____

_____

_____

Flashlight Button Christian

Sometimes I act like
A flashlight button Christian
Turning on that light
Only when I have a feelin'

I turn it off when I see
Someone that I don't want to talk to
I'm sure they aren't in need
And I wouldn't know what to do

When I see someone I know
I click the button again
The light comes on to show
I am a Christian

Walking down the street
I have my light off
Not knowing what I should be saying
Not wanting to have to stop

I go to church, or watch on-line
I have clicked the Christian flashlight button
Making sure that these people see that light shine
Not knowing the hypocrisy that is rotten

There it is... the flashlight button Christian
Push on the button when the time is right
Or when something might be missin'
Turn it off again when I don't want the light

So take my word and use some tape
Use some wire, just use something'
Hold that button down forever to make
Yourself not be a Flashlight Button Christian

Read:

- Matthew 6:1
- 2 Timothy 3:5
- Matthew 23:5
- Matthew 5:16

Do you ever turn your Christianity on or off depending on who is around?

_____

_____

_____

_____

_____

What line caught your attention most? What is it about those words you noticed?

_____

_____

_____

_____

_____

I'll Never Know

Sometimes the protection You are providing,
is not always known,
You have prevented accidents that aren't seen.

A tire that just missed a nail or screw in the road,
because of You,
how many incidents are avoided but still unknown?

A foot that just misses a wrong step,
an ankle not sprained,
will we ever know how much in You we are kept?

Eyes taken off the road looking at the scenery You made,
no oncoming cars,
without You we cannot make it home safe.

A sickness in the air misses a breath taken in deep,
a disease is missed,
the many times You keep us healthy remains a mystery.

I suppose it is not to know it all but just to be grateful,
the unknown avoided,
how much is prevented just because we remain faithful?

Read:

- Psalm 4:8
- Proverbs 19:23

What stands out to you the most?

_____

_____

_____

_____

Have you ever considered that you are protected from unknown or unseen things?

_____

_____

_____

_____

What changes can you make based on this information?

_____

_____

_____

One Day At A Time

Each morning is a new day-
I'm working on my attitude-
Changing some of my ways-
Doing my best to be like You.

I rebuke temptation-
Get away from me-
Using my redemption-
I fight the enemy.

I run this race-
Hour by hour-
Under Your grace-
By Your Power.

Wanting to obey You-
In Your love I remain-
Desiring to be used-
Serving You each day.

Every day is new-
Beautiful and divine-
Living it in You-
One day at a time.

Read:

- James 4:14
- Lamentations 3:22-23
- Psalm 118:24

Are you focused too much on what happened in the past? What is it that causes you to do that?

_____

_____

_____

_____

_____

_____

_____

_____

_____

What might help you remember to rejoice
in knowing that each day is new?

_____

_____

_____

_____

_____

You Are Enough

When things are going wrong
and life is super tough-
You are there and you are strong
and I know You are enough.

When I am feeling down and hopeless
with no chance and full of despair-
I long to feel Your closeness
and to know You are there.

Your presence is all it takes
to make this feeling change-
my insecurities are chased away
able to face another day.

Not my strength nor what I've done
helps me to carry on-
because You are enough
I can face it all.

Read:

- Philippians 4:13
- Deuteronomy 31:6

How often do you try and rely on your own strength?

_____

_____

_____

What is the outcome when you rely on your own strength?

_____

_____

_____

_____

_____

_____

_____

What can we learn from the passages read here?

_____

_____

_____

The Miraculous Fish

The crowd was hungry
getting angry

Following Jesus everywhere
hoping for food to share

He sat them on a hill
truths to instill

But they wanted food
the disciples saw the mood

A boy gave them a few fish
not hardly enough for one dish

But Jesus prayed
said grace with faith

Took the fish apart
handing it out to start

Everyone was satisfied
leftover baskets compiled

The miraculous fish fed a lot
the crowd content on the spot

The fish story shows
Jesus loved all of those

He knew their need
gave them something to eat

So, we know every minute, every hour
He sees the need of ours

He's willing with us to meet
give us what we need

Take your miraculous fish
and know that it was Jesus

Read:

- Luke 9:10-18
- Matthew 14:13-21

How does Jesus feeding the crowds relate to you?

_____

_____

_____

_____

What application can you make in reading about this miracle?

_____

_____

_____

Running With Jonah

I think I hear a voice-
maybe it's just a whispering.
Now I have to make a choice-
obey, or run like I didn't hear a thing.

Jonah took off fast when he heard
the task he was asked to do.
Not knowing what was about to occur
he went the opposite direction he was supposed to.

I feel myself tending to run with Jonah-
when I get scared or disagree with the plan.
I know a better way or think I can go it alone-
I'm sure my way is better and God will understand.

So off I run away from the right direction
hiding, wondering, gone from where I should go.
Safe here in my own protection
I stay with the way I chose.

Then I remember Jonah got swallowed-
into the belly of a giant whale.
Came out stinky and looking yellow-
he was not in the best of shape in his epic fail.

God gets my attention like that too-
then I come out smelly, gross, and nasty.
Sometimes that is what it takes to get through-
this thick head of mine to get me to see.

Thankfully, God never gives up-
even when I jump ship and fall away.
He is always there full of love-
ready to guide me back to His way.

Even though I run with Jonah every now and then
God is there to get my attention.
Bringing me to the task He has intended
and leading to a place of giving Him praises.

So when I feel myself start to run-
like Jonah did back then.
I remember that God called me to action-
and I turn around and follow Him.

Read:

- Jonah 1:3-4
- Jonah 1:16-18

**Have you ever caught yourself running from
God like Jonah did?**

_____

_____

_____

_____

_____

_____

_____

What caused you to turn back to God? Was it a "big fish?"

_____

_____

_____

_____

_____

_____

_____

Have you ever told anyone your "Jonah" story? Pray
God will give you the opportunity this week. Write out
what you might say to the next person with whom you
get to share your story.

_____

_____

_____

_____

_____

_____

_____

_____

_____

_____

The Despair Dumpster

Sometimes I feel like-
I've been tossed into despair-
it's dirty, damp, void of light-
feeling like no one cares-

The despair dumpster calls-
I hear nothing else-
Down I fall-
into this smelly mess-

Sometimes I climb in-
it's my own choice-
other times I'm tryin'-
to fight off the noise-

When I've hit the bottom-
no further down to go-
feeling like I'm rotten-
confidence is sittin pretty low-

But now.
I remember.
Somehow.
You are my defender.

I called out Your name-
You reached down in this pit-
no conviction, no shame-
hand offered for me to get-

I did this to myself alone-
yet here You are again-
rescuing me atoned-
from all my disgrace and sin-

Lifted out by Your hand-
with all joy to declare-
because of You I stand-
freed from this despair.

Read:

- Psalm 34:17-20
- 1 Peter 5:7

When do you feel despair set in?

_____

_____

_____

_____

_____

_____

_____

_____

_____

Do you recall moments when you called on Jesus to rescue you from that despair? How did Jesus help you out of the despair dumpster?

_____

_____

_____

_____

_____

_____

_____

What helps you remember Jesus is always there for you?

_____

_____

_____

_____

_____

_____

_____

_____

_____

_____

Crawlin' Up In My Daddy's Lap

I see my daddy, sittin' over there,
He looks so majestic, regal, and shiny.
I walk over to him, in his daddy chair,
He's smiling, beckoning, welcoming me.

He eagerly awaits; I reach my arms up to him,
carefully he reaches down and grabs a hold.
He sets me on his knee, looks at me and then,
hugs me tight; here I feel strong and bold.

He looks into my eyes with love,
there's never a look of disappointment here.
I get lost in his perfect look from above,
knowing there is a daddy's joy there.

This is a safe place for me,
no irritation or judgment found.
This is the place I love to be,
With my Daddy's arms all around.

Here I feel safe to ask any question,
knowing I can come openly and freely.
So when I wonder, I ask without reservation,
getting the perfect answer from my Daddy.

Read:

- Hebrews 4:16
- Jeremiah 29:13

What line or stanza stands out to you? Why?

_____

_____

_____

_____

_____

How does it feel to realize you can crawl up in God's lap?

_____

_____

_____

_____

_____

_____

The Sea That Opened Its Mouth

When Moses raised his staff over the water-
he never doubted that You would make a way.
The sea opened its mouth at Your order-
and the people passed on the dry land You made.

I want faith like that-
to raise my arms and split the sea.
So that is what I ask-
help me to live faithfully.

What faith!
All praise!

Give me a faith that is this strong-
split the seas of doubt residing in me.
Show up in a way that will not be forgotten-
drying up all my uncertainty.

I want faith that causes the sea to open its mouth-
not to use for selfish gain.
I want to show others what You are all about-
the spotlight on You every day.

That faith!
What to say!

Lead me in a way so that I can know-
that there is this faith available to me.
Then to the world I can show-
a faith that parts the seas.

Read:

- Exodus 14:26-29
- Matthew 17:20

At what times do you feel you need more faith?

_____

_____

_____

_____

_____

_____

_____

_____

How do feel knowing faith to part seas can be yours?

_____

_____

_____

_____

_____

_____

_____

_____

Divine Coffee Shop Hang Out

"Dear Lord, I kinda want a friend-
to hang out with while Christy's at work-
so I'm just asking that You send-
someone that will put up with my little quirks."

It happened, a friend showed up-
we decided to meet at a coffee shop-
we discovered we had lots in common-
we drank coffee and we talked

"Thank you, Lord, for this new friendship I have-
it's just what I needed without a doubt-
to sit around, drink coffee and chat-
quality time together just hanging out."

We are still friends even now-
we hang out together-
sometimes for coffee, or with our spouses
friends today, friends forever.

This is a divine intervention-
hanging out at a local coffee shop-
better than I ever could imagine-
talking over coffee at this special spot.

When have you met with a friend over coffee, or
dessert, or a meal and afterwards you knew it was
a divine appointment?

_____

_____

_____

_____

Do you pray for new friendships?

_____

_____

Do you look out for divine appointments that happen
in your life? Or, maybe you are looking for a coffee
shop friend. Write out a prayer to look for those new
friendships, or requesting new friends.

_____

_____

_____

_____

_____

_____

_____

Livin' In Joy

It's a new day.
Morning praise.
Hands raised.
Joy in waves.

Noon time now.
Joy all about.
Singin' out loud.
Praisin' in this house.

It's evening time.
Wonderful delight.
Still praising tonight.
Joy overflowing inside.

The day was enjoyed.
Even with some turmoil.
No difficulties preventing rejoicing.
I'm livin' in joy.

Read:

- Philippians 4:4
- Psalm 16:11
- Psalm 30:5
- Psalm 71:23

What stanzas or words spoke to you the most?

_____

_____

_____

_____

Why is important to remember to have joy every day?

_____

_____

_____

_____

How do you find your joy in the morning?

_____

_____

_____

_____

Baptized In Crick Water

Dedicated my life,
to my Savior-
Jesus Christ.

Next step,
Get baptized-
in a crick.

Yep, muddy water all around.
Fish, turtles, and snakes there.
Hearing the water's flowing sounds,
I stepped in the mud getting prepared.

The ground smished,
Unsteady legs-
Ready to be finished.

The pastor grabbed my hand,
and helped into the deep.
Water to my chest, could hardly stand,
he said a few words and sent me underneath.

Now dead to sin,
symbolically washed-
My life is His.

My eyes still closed.
Holding my breath.
Water going up my nose.
Had to be at least 40 seconds.

Then raised up,
a public expression-
of my inner transformation.

The dirty crick water,
had no magic properties.
It's all by the Spirit's power,
not some religiosity.

Follow Jesus, do what He did,
show the world-
your faith in Him.

Read:

- Matthew 3:16
- Galatians 3:26-27

Have you been baptized? If not, what is preventing you from the outward expression of your inward faith?

_____

_____

_____

_____

_____

_____

_____

_____

What Do I Have To Give?

I have just a few pennies,
I'm not super rich.
The pockets feel empty,
but I have a little I can give.

God, You don't really need my little bit,
You already own it all anyway.
So there's no harm if I go on and skip,
giving what You've asked of me today.

I know You don't want just my dollars and cents,
that's not what giving is all about.
I also need to give of my time and talents,
showing Your love to those around.

Selfishness seems to reign,
I want to hold back some for me.
I can't offer as much as others gave,
I'll just throw in a little, begrudgingly.

Then I hear a voice whisper to me,
"That is not what I'm about.
I don't need your money."
I stop and ask, who's that? I look around.

The spirit within continues to reassure,
"I just want your heart and will,
that is the real treasure."
Stopping, I get real still.

The spirit says to me,

"Give to me what you have today,
don't worry about other people.
It doesn't matter what those around you say,
you just follow My leading."

Then a sense of self-doubt rushes in,
I'm not super intelligent or talented.
I don't have the best time management,
what is there that I have to give?

His voice reassures me in this,
"All I want is you,
and your willingness.
I'll take care of the rest,
and I'll see you through."

So, I commit to giving what I have,
it's already all His.
I'm now willing to offer it back,
for that is what I have to give.

Read:

- 2 Corinthians 9:7
- Proverbs 3:9
- Hebrews 13:16

Do you give of your tithe, time, and talents?
Why or why not?

_____

_____

_____

_____

_____

_____

Does selfishness prevent you from being a cheerful
giver?

_____

_____

_____

How can you overcome this in your life?

_____

_____

_____

_____

_____

_____

I Will Stand Strong

God is my Redeemer,
He has overcome the world.
He is always with me,
He is the One I serve.

Even though trouble comes,
His strength reigns in me.
I will resist any temptation,
and stand in victory.

Greater is He that lives forever,
than anything else I encounter.
I will live in His power,
every minute of every hour.

His strength is how I stand,
being led and guided,
by His loving hand.

His name is my life's song,
I sing it all day long.

I will stand strong!

Read:

- Psalm 31:24
- Proverbs 28:7

How can you better allow Jesus' strength to reign in you?

_____

_____

_____

_____

_____

_____

Write out a statement of faith, standing strong in Jesus' redemption power and strength.

_____

_____

_____

_____

_____

_____

_____

_____

Leaving A Legacy

Do you ever think about,
the legacy you are leaving?
This is no doubt,
for your family.

After all you've been through,
and even at this point in your life-
do they see Jesus in you,
are you leaving a legacy of this kind?

Consider more than just wealth and gain,
know there are those coming after you.
This may not sound like the world's way,
but leaving a legacy is a good thing to do.

And let it be known here and now,
this is not just any ole legacy.
This is one of goodness and love,
one that everyone should see.

Do not let your legacy be,
one of selfishness and greed.
Show a life of love and mercy,
and leave a Godly legacy.

Read:

- Psalm 78:4
- Psalm 145:4
- Matthew 6:20-21

What kind of legacy are you leaving for your family?

_____

_____

_____

_____

_____

_____

After these last 89 days of devotions, what changes
do you plan to make to leave a Godly legacy?

_____

_____

_____

_____

_____

_____

_____

_____

Thank you so much for joining me on this 90-day journey. My prayer is that you gained insight, grew closer to God, and heard the Holy Spirit speak to you.

Thanks again so much for walking through the last 90-days with me. May God bless you and bless you more abundantly!

I would love to hear about how this book had an impact on your life. Please leave a review for the book letting me know your favorite poems, and how these devotionals helped you.

.

Printed in Great Britain
by Amazon

75803665R00132